IMAGES OF
ST. IVES

Photographed by John Curtis

SALMON

INTRODUCTION

Crystal clear, blue waters and long stretches of golden, sandy beaches surround St. Ives, one of Cornwall's most popular seaside resorts. Situated on St. Ives Bay in the far west of the county, facing the wind and the waves of the Atlantic, St. Ives has become a favoured haunt of artists and writers, as well as holiday-makers. Once a busy fishing village exporting fish to faraway destinations, it became one of Cornwall's most prosperous ports and the harbour is still home to fishing boats, which land their catch of fresh fish and shellfish here each day. Around the harbour is the old town with its picturesque colour-washed fishermen's cottages which crowd together in the narrow, cobbled streets behind the quay. This picturesque setting, coupled with the fabled quality of the light, have attracted artists to St. Ives for more than two hundred years. Turner found inspiration for a landscape painting here in 1811, but it was in the 1920s that the artists' colony, we still see here today, was first founded. Ben Nicholson and Dame Barbara Hepworth moved to St. Ives in the late 1930s, and in the decades since then, an increasing number of galleries and artists' studios have sprung up, culminating in the opening of the Tate St. Ives in 1993. This vibrant artistic community has done much to preserve the individual character of the town, and to attract the discerning visitor, while the excellent beaches that line the coast, including Porthmeor Beach to the north of the town, which offers the best surfing conditions, and Porthminster Beach to the south-east, a safe haven for families, makes St. Ives the perfect holiday destination.

The Harbour
Backed by the busy quayside, the harbour always presents a scene of great activity, and, in summer, sheltered Harbour Beach is thronged with holiday-makers.

The Sloop Inn
Set right on the harbour front, the picturesque Sloop Inn is one of Cornwall's most ancient and famous inns, believed to date from around 1312.

St. Leonard's Chapel
Tiny St. Leonard's Chapel stands on the landward end of Smeaton's Pier, and was traditionally where the local fishermen would say their prayers before going out to sea.

Bamaluz Beach
The small, sandy beach, known as Bamaluz, is tucked in just below St. Ives Museum, and its sheltered location makes it known locally as the 'secret beach'.

Smeaton's Pier

The harbour is protected by a handsome stone pier, built in 1770 by John Smeaton. It was largely thanks to this pier, and the shelter it provided, that St. Ives was able to flourish as a port in the 19th century. The impressive stone breakwater was extended in the late 1890s, leaving the original lighthouse halfway along its length.

Porthgwidden Beach
Although it is the smallest of several fine beaches in the town, Porthgwidden is one of the most popular with holiday-makers because of its safe bathing and its sheltered, sunny aspect. It is protected from the wind by St. Ives Head, a grassy promontory known locally as The Island.

The Island
Separating Porthmeor Beach from Porthgwidden, The Island peninsula juts out into St. Ives Bay. On the top stands restored St. Nicholas's Chapel, which was once reputedly used by smugglers as a look-out.

Porthmeor Beach
The glorious sands of Porthmeor Beach and the clear waters of the bay are a perennial favourite with visitors and surfers alike, who flock to the town in the summer.

Tate St. Ives
Testiment to St. Ives' popularity with artists and art lovers alike, this striking building houses a branch of the famous Tate Gallery and features the work of many local artists.

Old St. Ives

The picturesque Old Town with its charming colour-washed stone fishermen's cottages crowded together in cobbled streets and narrow alleyways, is nestled around the old harbour. Redolent with history and tradition, many houses date from the 18th century and the streets are a labyrinth of galleries, restaurants and little shops. Behind the Sloop Inn is the Sloop Craft Workshops (left) with its delightful craft market and a collection of artists' studios.

Church of St. Ia, St. Peter and St. Andrew

The parish church of St. Ives dominates the skyline of the Old Town and is dedicated to the missionary St. Ia who, according to legend, sailed into the bay on a leaf in the 5th or 6th century. The Lady Chapel was added between 1450 and 1500 and contains a Madonna and Child carving by the sculptor Barbara Hepworth, while the nave features a beautifully carved barrel roof. A weathered 15th century stone cross outside the south porch features God the Father upholding the crucified Christ.

Barbara Hepworth Museum and Sculpture Garden

Like so many other artists, Dame Barbara Hepworth found her spiritual home in St. Ives. From 1949 until her death in 1975, she lived and worked at Trewyn Studios, now the Hepworth Museum. Her former home creates a very personal setting for her work, which is displayed to great effect in the house and the sculpture garden.

Trewyn Garden

Beautiful Trewyn Garden is a hidden oasis in the middle of town. With its colourful borders, flowering shrubs and exotic trees, it demonstrates why St. Ives continues to be a winner of the 'Britain in Bloom' award.

The Guildhall
The work of the great sculptress and local resident, Dame Barbara Hepworth, can be enjoyed in several places around St. Ives. This great bronze entitled, 'Dual Form', stands on the steps outside the handsome Guildhall.

The Memorial Garden
Subtropical plants and tender flowers flourish in the gardens of St. Ives which is known for its temperate climate and early springs. The delightful Memorial Garden provides a peaceful haven in the heart of the town.

Carbis Bay
The golden sands of Carbis Bay lie sheltered beneath a steep, wooded hillside, which provides excellent cliff walks, and the rocks are a popular spot for fishermen.

Porthminster Beach
Backed by attractive lawns and gardens, the town's longest beach is Porthminster Beach; sheltered by St. Ives Head, it offers good bathing in the calm waters.

Porth Kidney Sands
A gloriously huge expanse of beach stretching from Hawkes Point to the mouth of the River Hayle, Porth Kidney Sands lie not far from the village of Lelant.

St. Uny's Church, Lelant
This romantic 15th century church is dedicated to St. Uny and stands prominently on the edge of the dunes at Lelant, looking out over the mouth of the River Hayle.

Godrevy Island

Three miles of beautiful sands sweep up the coast from Hayle towards Godrevy Point, a headland protected by The National Trust. The rock-strewn channel between Godrevy Island and the Point claimed many lives before the lighthouse was built in 1859.

The Bucket of Blood Inn, Phillack

This rather macabre sounding inn is to be found in the little village of Phillack, just north of Hayle. Legend has it that in the days of smuggling, the landlord hoisted up a bucket of blood from his well, revealing the murdered body of a customs officer at the bottom.

Knill Monument
John Knill was the slightly eccentric collector of customs in St. Ives, who later became the town's mayor. This mausoleum was built by Knill himself in 1782 and stands high on Worvas Hill overlooking Carbis Bay. The town has celebrated John Knill Day every five years on July 25th since 1801.

Giew Mine, Cripplesease
In the 19th century, Cornwall was the centre of an extensive tin and copper mining industry. This old engine house in the little hamlet of Cripplesease serves as a monument to this heritage.

Zennor

Situated between the towering cliffs and the hills, the village of Zennor lies on a coastal plateau which has been cultivated since the Iron Age. The 12th century church is dedicated to the little known Saint Senara, believed to have been a Breton princess who was miraculously saved from drowning. Another legend has it that a local man, who sang in the church, fell in love with a beautiful mermaid, and followed her into the water, never to be seen again. A bench end, some six hundred years old, with a beautifully carved mermaid, can be seen in the church.

Published by J. Salmon Ltd., Sevenoaks, Kent TN13 1BB. © 2009
Website: www.jsalmon.co.uk Telephone: 01732 452381. Email: enquiries@jsalmon.co.uk.

Design and photographs by John Curtis © John Curtis.

All rights reserved. No part of this book may be produced, stored in a retrieval system or transmitted in any form or by any means without prior written permission of the publishers.

Acknowledgement: Special thanks to Bowness, Hepworth Estate for permission to photograph at the Barbara Hepworth Museum, St. Ives and to the staff for their generous assistance.

ISBN 978-1-84640-184-8

Title page photograph: Window in Lelant Church Half title page: Low tide in the harbour
Front cover photograph: St. Ives from the rooftops Back cover photograph: The quay at night
Page 32 photograph: Sunset across St. Ives Bay

Salmon Books

ENGLISH IMAGES SERIES

Photography by John Curtis

Titles available in this series

English Abbeys and Priories	English Country Pubs
English Gardens	English Castles
English Country Towns	English Cathedrals
English Cottages	English Country Churches
English Landscape Gardens	Jane Austen's England
English Follies	Romantic England
English Villages	Mysterious England